State of Vermont
Department of Libraries
Northeast Regional Library
RD 2
Box 244
St. Johnsbury, VT 05819

A Groundwood Book
Douglas and McIntyre
Toronto, Vancouver

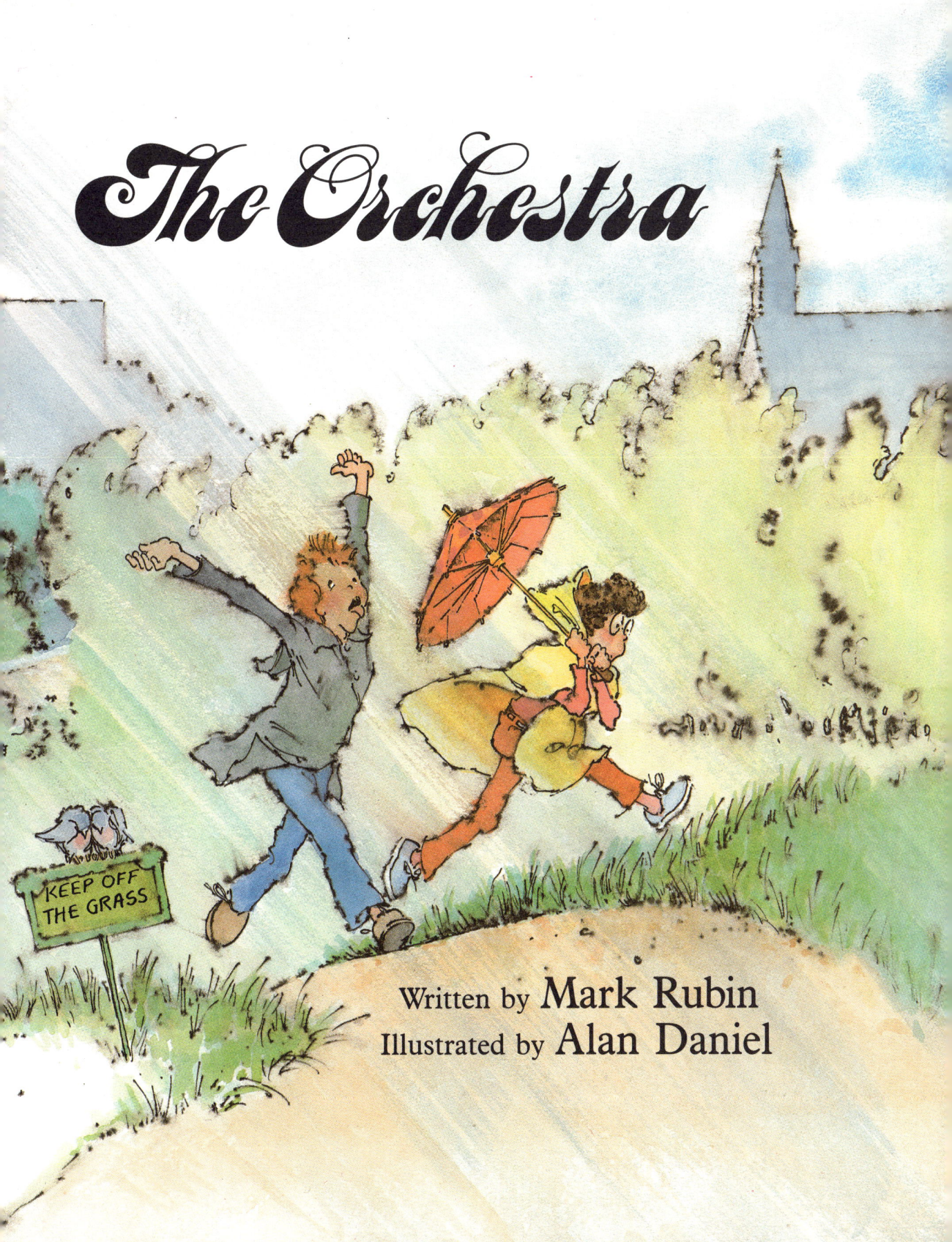

Music is everywhere. It is in the sound of the wind, the singing of birds, the patter of rain.

All of these sounds are parts of Nature's music.

People make music by singing, or by playing musical instruments.
  Someone who has learned to sing or to play an instrument well is called a MUSICIAN.

There are many kinds of musicians,
many kinds of instruments,
many kinds of music.

Music can sound happy, or it can sound sad. It can sound exciting, or it can sound peaceful. It can sound serious, or it can sound silly.

Music can sound as many different ways as you can feel.

Sometimes music tells a story. Sometimes music is just interesting sound. Sometimes music makes you want to jump up and dance. Sometimes it makes you want to sit quietly and listen.

Music can sound like almost anything you can imagine.

Making up music is called COMPOSING. The person who makes up the music is called the COMPOSER.

The composer writes down musical ideas using musical pictures called notes. There are high notes, low notes, everywhere-in-between notes. Every note stands for a certain musical sound.

When composing a piece of music the composer must think of many things.

First the composer must find a certain arrangement of notes to form the music's MELODY. The melody is the most familiar part of the music—the part you can hum.

Next the composer may add some
other notes that go with the melody.
These notes are called the HARMONY.

Then the composer must give the music RHYTHM. Rhythm is the way the music moves and flows. Like the ticking of a clock, the music must have a steady BEAT. Like the beating of your heart, some of the beats may be stronger than others.

The composer still has other important choices to make.
    Should the music be fast, or slow, or somewhere in between? The speed at which the music is played is called its TEMPO.

Finally, the composer must decide which instruments will play which parts of the music. This gives the music its TONE COLOUR. The same music can sound very different played on different instruments.

All of these choices must be made very carefully, if the music is to turn out just as the composer wants it to.

The composer has the most choices when the music is for an ORCHESTRA with its many different instruments and many musicians.

There are four main groups of instruments in an orchestra — the string instruments, the woodwind instruments, the brass instruments, and the percussion instruments.

Each of these groups is called a FAMILY, because all of its instruments are related to each other in important ways.

The STRING FAMILY is by far the largest in the orchestra. All of the string family's instruments have strings on them. To play a string instrument the player either moves a bow across one of the strings, or plucks it with a finger.

The bow or player's finger makes the string VIBRATE. When the string vibrates it makes a sound.

The player can play different notes by holding down the strings in different places.

When the player presses on a string it makes the vibrating part of the string shorter. The shorter the vibrating string, the higher the sound; the longer the vibrating string, the lower the sound.

The VIOLIN is the smallest member of the string family, but it is very important because it often plays the melody.

There are more violins in the orchestra than any other instrument.

The VIOLA looks just like the violin, but it is a little bit bigger and sounds a little bit lower.

The CELLO is too big to be held under the chin like the violin and viola. It must rest on the floor between the player's knees.

The DOUBLE BASS is so big that most players stand up to play it. It is the largest member of the string family. Because it is so big and its strings are so long, its sound is very, very low.

All the instruments of the WOODWIND FAMILY
are narrow tubes with a row of holes
in them. Most of them are made of wood.

Woodwind instruments are played by blowing into them. The wind of the player's breath makes the air inside the instrument vibrate. The vibrating air makes the sound.

To play different notes on a woodwind instrument the player covers different holes with the fingers. The more holes that are covered, the longer the column of air vibrating inside, and the lower the sound.

To play the OBOE, the player blows between two thin pieces of wood. These pieces of wood are called REEDS.

When the player blows, the reeds vibrate very rapidly. This is what gives the oboe its special sound.

There is an instrument called the ENGLISH HORN. But it isn't English, and it isn't a horn! It's really a woodwind quite like the oboe, except it is a little larger, and has an egg-shaped bulge on its end.

The BASSOON is a very long tube folded in half to make it easier to hold and play.

The bassoon has a double reed like the oboe and English horn, but because the bassoon is much longer, its sound is much lower.

The DOUBLE BASSOON, or CONTRABASSOON, is twice as long as the bassoon. Its tube is folded over twice. The double bassoon is so long it can play the lowest notes in the whole orchestra.

The CLARINET looks a lot like the oboe. But instead of a double reed, the clarinet has only one reed attached to a mouthpiece.

The FLUTE is different from the other woodwinds. It used to be made of wood a long time ago, but today most flutes are made of silver metal. The flute is also different because it is held sideways instead of up and down, and because it is played by blowing across an open hole.

The PICCOLO is a tiny flute. It is so small and so short it can play the highest notes.

The BRASS FAMILY'S instruments are all made of brass — a shiny gold-coloured metal. They are all long tubes which are bent and twisted into shapes that make them easier to hold and play.

Like the woodwinds, the brass instruments are played by blowing into them. But the brass have no reeds, so to make the air vibrate, the player must blow and make a buzzing with the lips at the same time.

To play the different notes the brass player presses on VALVES with the fingers. Pressing a valve changes the length of the column of air vibrating inside.

The TROMBONE doesn't have valves like the other brass instruments. Instead it has a sliding section of tubing which the player moves in and out.

The biggest brass instrument is the TUBA. It has over nine metres of tubing in it! With such a long column of air, the tuba can play notes that are very low.

Instruments of the PERCUSSION FAMILY are played by being struck or shaken. This makes the instrument vibrate, which makes the sound.

Some of the percussion instruments are used mainly for rhythm, like the SNARE DRUM and the BASS DRUM. Others are used mainly for their special sound, like the CYMBALS, TRIANGLE, TAMBOURINE, and GONG.

A few of the percussion instruments can play different notes, like the XYLOPHONE, GLOCKENSPIEL, and CHIMES.

The KETTLEDRUMS, or TIMPANI, are like giant bowls, with a thin covering stretched over the top.
 There are usually four kettledrums in an orchestra. One player plays them all. Each kettledrum can be tuned to play a different note.

The PIANO is a very special instrument. It has a KEYBOARD with 88 keys on it. Inside the piano are 88 little wooden hammers, and many wire strings. When the player presses on a key, it moves a hammer, which strikes certain strings. The player can press several keys at the same time.

The piano doesn't always play with the orchestra, but when it does it usually has an important part.

The CELESTE looks like a little piano. But instead of wire strings inside, it has metal bars. They give the celeste its bell-like sound.

Another unusual instrument is the HARP. The harp has forty-seven strings of different lengths. Each string sounds a different note.

The harp is played by plucking or brushing it with the fingers.

Finally, there is one last member of the orchestra who is very, very important. This is the CONDUCTOR.

The conductor is the person who guides the musicians as they are playing so that everyone will play together perfectly.

Holding a little stick called a BATON in the right hand, the conductor shows the musicians the tempo and rhythm of the music to be played.

With the left hand, the conductor points to different parts of the orchestra as it is their turn to play.

Using both hands, and face, and the whole body the conductor expresses the feelings with which the orchestra should play.

After the conductor and all the musicians have practised together for a long time, the orchestra is ready to perform its music in a CONCERT.

The audience fills the concert hall. The musicians tune their instruments. The conductor enters to thunderous applause.

The conductor raises the baton, and for a moment all is quiet.

Then the baton swooshes down . . .

. . . and the orchestra's music begins.